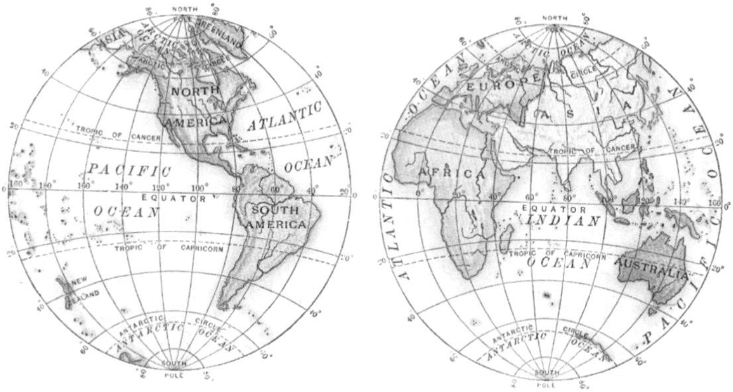
NORTH POLE
ASIA
ARCTIC OCEAN
GREENLAND
ARCTIC CIRCLE
NORTH AMERICA
ATLANTIC OCEAN
TROPIC OF CANCER
PACIFIC OCEAN
EQUATOR
SOUTH AMERICA
TROPIC OF CAPRICORN
NEW ZEALAND
ANTARCTIC CIRCLE
ANTARCTIC OCEAN
SOUTH POLE
EUROPE
ASIA
AFRICA
INDIAN OCEAN
AUSTRALIA
PACIFIC OCEAN
ATLANTIC OCEAN

House Flags and Funnels
OF THE
PRINCIPAL TRANSATLANTIC S.S. COS.
CUNARD LINE
HAMBURG AMERICAN
ALLAN LINE
ANCHOR LINE
NORTH GER LLOYD S.S. CO.
FRENCH LINE
HOLLAND AM. LINE
RED STAR LINE
AMERICAN LINE
WILSON LINE
WHITE STAR LINE
THINGVALLA LINE
JOHNSTON LINE
LEYLAND LINE
ATLANTIC LINE
LAMPORT-HOLT LINE
BEAVER LINE
WILSON FURNESS-LEYLAND-LINE
BRISTOL CITY LINE
DOMINION LINE
FABRE LINE
FLORIO LINE
MANHANSET LINE
ATLANTIC TRANSPORT LINE
SCANDINAVIAN AM. LINE
MEDITERRANEAN LINE
NATIONAL LINE
PHOENIX LINE
WARREN LINE
ARROW LINE
BORDEAUX LINE
UNION LINE
COPYRIGHT 1901 BY BRENTANO'S

Destinations

CHRONICLE BOOKS

In memory of Edith Van Santvoordt,
and with many thanks to Nate Scoble.

ISBN: 0-8118-2497-7

Manufactured in China
This book is typeset in Electra.
Distributed in Canada by
Raincoast Books
9050 Shaughnessy Street
Vancouver, B.C. V6P 6E5

10 9 8 7

Chronicle Books LLC
85 Second Street
San Francisco, CA 94105
www.chroniclebooks.com

Concept and design: Gretchen Scoble
Handlettering by Nancy Stentz

This book belongs to:

. . . .

Personal Information

Name . . . .

Address . . . .

. . . .

Telephone . . . .

Fax . . . .

Mobile . . . .

E-Mail . . . .

Passport No. . . . .

In case of emergency please notify:

Name . . . .

Address . . . .

. . . .

Telephone . . . .

Outward Bound

Departing from: ....

Via: ....

Date: ....

Time of departure: ....

Time of arrival: ....

Men are the merriest when they are far from home.

—William Shakespeare

Travel Map of EUROPE
0° Longitude East from Greenwich
British Isles
GREAT BRITAIN
SCOTLAND
ENGLAND
WALES
IRELAND
London
Dublin
Edinburgh
Glasgow
Liverpool
Manchester
North Sea
English Channel
Bay of Biscay
NORWAY
SWEDEN
DENMARK
Kristiania
Stockh
Copenhagen
Gulf of Bothnia
Baltic Sea
NETHERLANDS (HOLLAND)
BELGIUM
Brussels
GERMAN EMPIRE
Berlin
Hamburg
Munich
FRANCE
Paris
SWITZERLAND
Bern
AUSTRIA
Vienna
ITALY
Rome
Naples
Milan
Corsica (To France)
Sardinia
Sicily
Adriatic Sea
Tyrrhenian Sea
SPAIN
Madrid
Barcelona
Balearic Islands
MEDITERRANEAN SEA
Gibraltar (Br.)
Ceuta (Sp.)
Algiers

Itinerary

DATE: NOTES:

Itinerary

DATE: NOTES:

Itinerary

Date:	Notes:
....	....
....	....
....	....
....	....
....	....
....	....
....	....
....	....
....	....
....	....
....	....
....	....
....	....
....	....
....	....
....	....
....	....
....	....
....	....
....	....

Itinerary

DATE: NOTES:

Itinerary

DATE: NOTES:

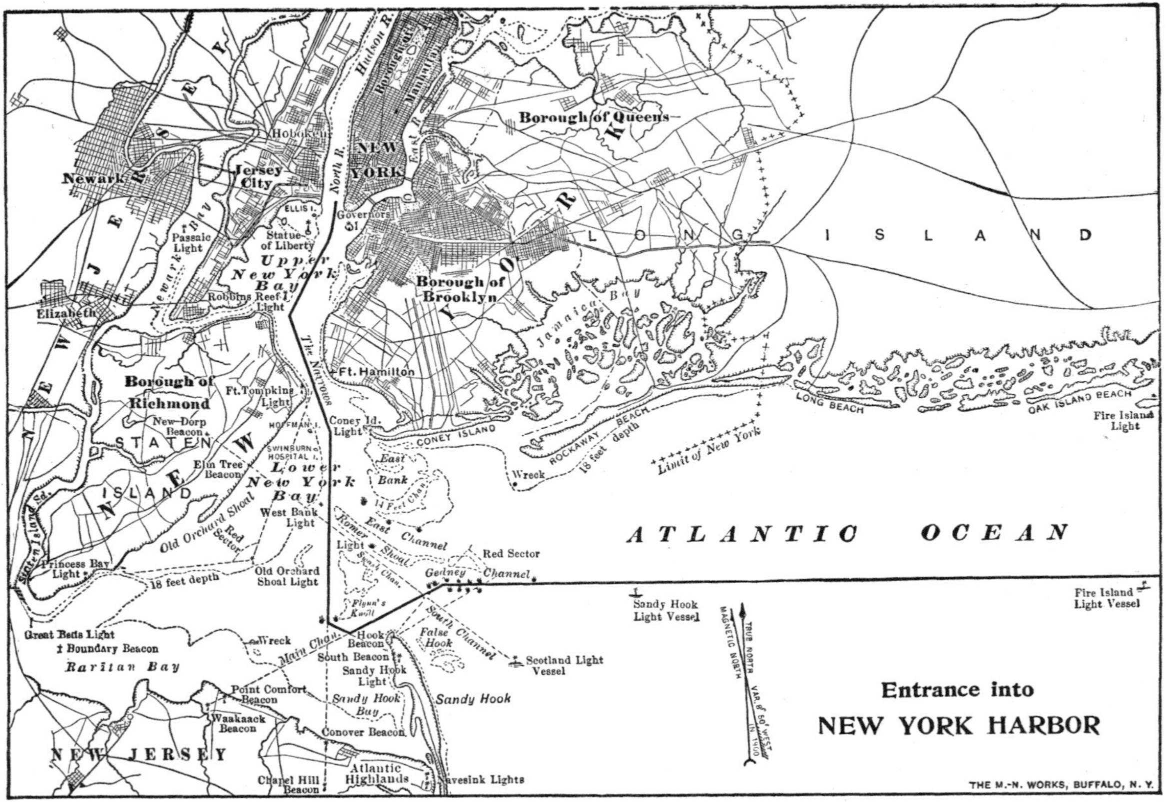
Entrance into
NEW YORK HARBOR
THE M.-N. WORKS, BUFFALO, N. Y.
ATLANTIC OCEAN
LONG ISLAND
NEW YORK
NEW JERSEY
Borough of Queens
Borough of Brooklyn
Borough of Manhattan
Borough of Richmond
STATEN ISLAND
Newark
Jersey City
Hoboken
Elizabeth
Hudson R.
North R.
East R.
Governors I.
Ellis I.
Statue of Liberty
Upper New York Bay
Lower New York Bay
Passaic Light
Newark Bay
Robbins Reef Light
The Narrows
Ft. Hamilton
Ft. Tompkins Light
Hoffman I.
Swinburne Hospital I.
Coney Id. Light
Coney Island
New-Dorp Beacon
Elm Tree Beacon
West Bank Light
Old Orchard Shoal
Red Sector
Old Orchard Shoal Light
Princess Bay Light
Staten Island Sd.
18 feet depth
Jamaica Bay
Rockaway Beach
Long Beach
Oak Island Beach
Fire Island Light
Limit of New York
Wreck
East Bank
14 Feet Chan.
East Channel
Romer Shoal
Swash Chan.
Gedney Channel
Flynn's Knoll
South Channel
False Hook
Hook Beacon
South Beacon
Sandy Hook Light
Sandy Hook Bay
Sandy Hook
Main Chan.
Scotland Light Vessel
Sandy Hook Light Vessel
Fire Island Light Vessel
True North
Magnetic North
Var. 8° 50' West in 1900
Great Beds Light
Boundary Beacon
Raritan Bay
Point Comfort Beacon
Waakaack Beacon
Conover Beacon
Atlantic Highlands
Chapel Hill Beacon
Navesink Lights

Metric Conversions

Weight

1 ounce = 28.35 grams

1 gram = .035 ounce

1 pound = .454 kilogram

1 kilogram = 2.2 pounds

Length/Distance

1 inch = 25.4 millimeters or 2.54 centimeters

1 centimeter = .394 inch

1 foot = .3 meter

1 meter = 3.28 feet

1 mile = 1.61 kilometers

1 kilometer = .62 mile

Liquid Measure

1 pint = .473 liter

1 quart = .46 liter

1 gallon = 3.785 liters

Temperature

32° Fahrenheit = 0° Celsius or Centigrade

0° Fahrenheit = -17.8° Celsius or Centigrade

Formulas for converting temperatures:

To convert Celsius to Fahrenheit, multiply by 9/5 and add 32.

To convert Fahrenheit to Celsius, subtract 32 and multiply by 5/9.

The International Signal Code

INTERNATIONAL CODE OF SIGNALS FOR SHIPS communicating with each other at sea or with stations on shore: a, the letter *A*; hoisted under the ensign it becomes the *"code signal"* signifying that a message is to be sent—the receiving ship hoists it conspicuously as the *"answering pennant—"* b, the letter *B*; c, the letter *C*, and the sign for assent, *"YES;"* d, the letter *D*, and negative sign, *"NO;"* f, g, h, k, l, m, n, p, the letters indicated; *P*, serves also as a pilot-flag in many cases; q, the letter *Q*, and sign for *quarantine*; r, the letter *R*; s, with blue square, the letter *S*; with red square, ss, the special flag of the signal service; t, v, w, the letters indicated. Vowels (except *a*) have no code signal.

Distance signals combining Balls and Flags used when the "Code" cannot be read: 1, the letter *C*; also means *"Yes."* 2, letter *B*; also asks name of a vessel or semaphore. 3, letter *F*. 4, letter *R*; also *"Report me by telegraph."* 5, letter *L*; also *"Pilot wanted."* 6, letter *D*; also *"No."* 7, special signal signifying *"In want of food."* 8, letter *G*; also *"Cannot make out your flags; make distance-signals."* 9, special signal signifying *"Aground; want help."* 10, the letter *K*; also asks for dispatches. 11, the letter *F*; also *"Repeat signal or hoist in a more conspicuous place."*

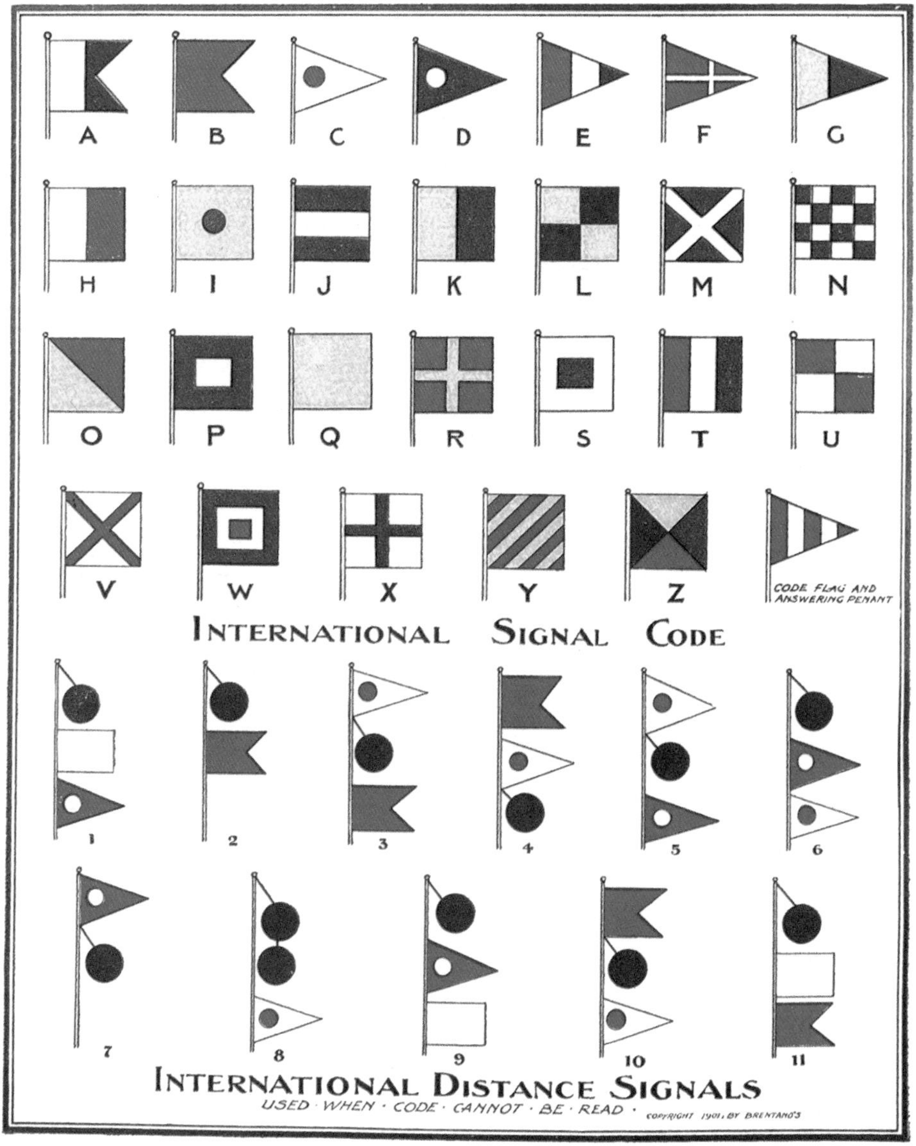
A
B
C
D
E
F
G
H
I
J
K
L
M
N
O
P
Q
R
S
T
U
V
W
X
Y
Z
CODE FLAG AND ANSWERING PENANT
INTERNATIONAL SIGNAL CODE
1
2
3
4
5
6
7
8
9
10
11
INTERNATIONAL DISTANCE SIGNALS
USED · WHEN · CODE · CANNOT · BE · READ ·
COPYRIGHT 1901, BY BRENTANO'S

STANDARD TIME WHEN NOON IN NEW YORK CITY
NEW YORK
ANTWERP
CITY OF MEXICO
BERLIN
BRUSSELS
BREMEN
CONSTANTINOPEL
GENEVA
COPENHAGEN
EDINBURGH
DUBLIN
HAMBURG
JERUSALEM
HAVANA
HONGKONG
NEXT DAY
LIVERPOOL
PANAMA
MADRID
LONDON
MELBOURNE
NEXT DAY
PARIS
YOKOHAMA
NEXT DAY
ROME
PETERSBURG
VIENNA

International Dialing Codes

Algeria	213	Guyana	592	Niger	227
Antigua	268	Haiti	509	Norway	47
Argentina	54	Honduras	504	Pakistan	92
Australia	61	Hong Kong	852	Panama	507
Austria	43	Hungary	36	Paraguay	595
Bahamas	242	Iceland	354	Peru	51
Belgium	32	India	91	Philippines	63
Belize	501	Indonesia	62	Poland	48
Bermuda	441	Ireland	353	Portugal	351
Bolivia	591	Israel	972	Puerto Rico	787
Brazil	55	Italy	39	Russia	7
Canada	1	Ivory Coast	225	Senegal	221
Chile	56	Jamaica	876	Singapore	65
China (PRC)	86	Japan	81	Slovak Republic	421
Costa Rica	506	Kenya	254	Slovenia	386
Cyprus	357	Korea (North)	850	South Africa	27
Czech Republic	420	Korea (South)	82	Spain	34
Denmark	45	Luxembourg	352	Sweden	46
Ecuador	593	Madagascar	261	Switzerland	41
Egypt	20	Malaysia	60	Taiwan	886
Fiji Islands	679	Martinique	596	Thailand	66
Finland	358	Mexico	52	Trinidad & Tobago	868
France	33	Monaco	377	Tunisia	216
French Polynesia	689	Montserrat	664	Turkey	90
Germany	49	Morocco	212	United Kingdom	44
Greece	30	Mozambique	258	USA	1
Greenland	299	Nepal	977	US Virgin Islands	1
Guadeloupe	590	Netherlands	599	Venezuela	58
Guatemala	502	New Zealand	64	Yugoslavia	381

Names & Addresses

Name	Address

Names & Addresses

NAME	ADDRESS
. . . .	. . . .
. . . .	. . . .
. . . .	. . . .
. . . .	. . . .
. . . .	. . . .
. . . .	. . . .
. . . .	. . . .
. . . .	. . . .
. . . .	. . . .
. . . .	. . . .
. . . .	. . . .
. . . .	. . . .
. . . .	. . . .
. . . .	. . . .
. . . .	. . . .
. . . .	. . . .
. . . .	. . . .
. . . .	. . . .
. . . .	. . . .
. . . .	. . . .

Names & Addresses

Name	Address

Names & Addresses

Name	Address

Names & Addresses

Name	Address
....	....
....	....
....	....
....	....
....	....
....	....
....	....
....	....
....	....
....	....
....	....
....	....
....	....
....	....
....	....
....	....
....	....
....	....
....	....
....	....

Names & Addresses

Name	Address
....	....
....	....
....	....
....	....
....	....
....	....
....	....
....	....
....	....
....	....
....	....
....	....
....	....
....	....
....	....
....	....
....	....
....	....
....	....
....	....

Hotels Where I Stayed

City	Hotel
....	....
....	....
....	....
....	....
....	....
....	....
....	....
....	....
....	....
....	....
....	....
....	....
....	....
....	....
....	....
....	....
....	....
....	....
....	....

Hotels Where I Stayed

City	Hotel

Restaurants I Enjoyed

City	Name

Restaurants I Enjoyed

City	Name

Restaurants I Enjoyed

City	Name

Restaurants I Enjoyed

City	Name

Shopping & Gifts

Shopping & Gifts

Shopping & Gifts

Shopping & Gifts

The Game of Shuffleboard

SHUFFLEBOARD IS THE GOLF OF SHIPBOARD. This ancient and interesting game is familiar to nearly every ocean traveler. Many an otherwise tedious hour has been merrily passed with shuffleboard.

The game is played in the following manner: A diagram, similar to the one shown, is chalked on the deck, covering a space about thirty square feet. The weights are wooden and pushed from a distance of nine or ten paces. The players use a staff with a curved end to push the weights. Each one plays in turn, but there is no scoring until the finish of the round, when the players are credited with the number of points marked in the square occupied by their weights. An opponent's piece may be struck out of the square altogether and a friend's pushed in by being hit with the piece of a following player.

Should a weight remain in the semicircular space nearest the players, ten is deducted from that player's score. To win the game a player must score exactly fifty points; all points over that number are subtracted from fifty. For example: Should a player's score be forty-seven, and he scores six points more, three would be added to make his count fifty and the other three deducted, which would still leave the score forty-seven.

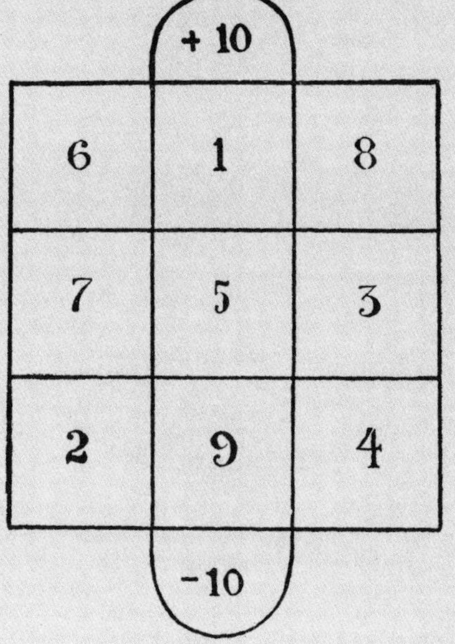

DIAGRAM OF SHUFFLEBOARD

Climates Around the World

[TEMPERATURES ARE IN DEGREES FAHRENHEIT]

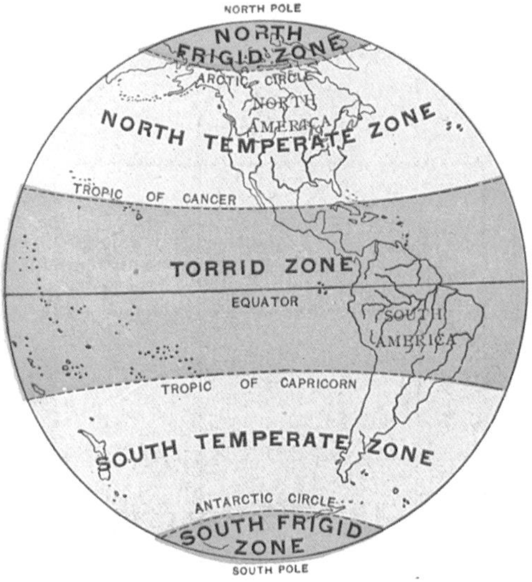

LOCATION	SPRING [Mar-May]	SUMMER [June-Aug]	FALL [Sept-Nov]	WINTER [Dec-Feb]
Acapulco	81°	84°	82°	80°
Athens	61	81	67	53
Auckland	60	51	56	64
Bangkok	85	84	82	79
Barcelona	58	74	63	50
Berlin	47	64	48	32
Bermuda	66	78	74	64
Budapest	53	70	52	32
Buenos Aires	62	51	61	73
Cairo	70	82	74	59
Caracas	78	76	76	75
Chicago	50	73	56	28

Location	Spring *[Mar-May]*	Summer *[June-Aug]*	Fall *[Sept-Nov]*	Winter *[Dec-Feb]*
Dublin	64°	81°	66°	46°
Edinburgh	45	57	48	38
Florence	56	74	59	43
Geneva	49	65	50	34
Hong Kong	71	82	76	61
Honolulu	74	78	78	72
Jerusalem	60	74	68	49
Istanbul	53	72	60	44
Kathmandu	43	75	67	52
Lisbon	58	70	63	52
London	51	64	55	43
Los Angeles	61	70	66	57
Madrid	55	73	58	43
Manila	84	83	82	79
Marseille	55	71	59	45
Mexico City	64	63	59	56
Miami	75	82	77	68
Moscow	39	63	40	16
Munich	46	62	46	30
Nairobi	66	60	64	65
New York City	50	73	56	33
Paris	50	64	52	38
Rio de Janeiro	75	70	72	78
Rome	57	74	62	46
San Francisco	55	59	59	50
Seattle	50	63	52	41
Seoul	51	75	55	28
Singapore	82	81	81	80
Stockholm	39	61	44	27
Sydney	35	61	48	24
Taipei	70	82	74	60
Tokyo	55	75	62	41
Toronto	43	67	49	25
Vancouver	48	62	50	39
Venice	54	72	56	38
Zurich	47	63	48	32

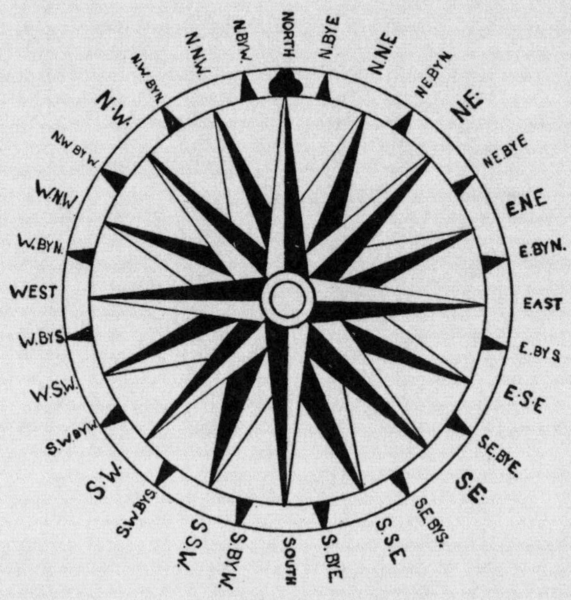

THE MARINER'S COMPASS

The Mariner's Compass

THE COMPASS IS USED TO INDICATE the magnetic meridian or the position of objects with reference to the meridian. Its chief forms are the mariner's azimuth and variation compass. The essentials of these are the same and consist of, first, a magnetic needle balanced on a point and capable of turning in a horizontal plane and second, a circular disk, either attached to the needle and turning with it or fixed in position and placed below the needle as in the azimuth.

The disk is graduated around its circumference into thirty-two divisions, each divided into halves and quarters and called the points of the compass.

The iron used in the construction of the ship, elements of magnetism in the cargo, the machinery, wire shrouds, boat davits, smokestack, etc., all tend to bring about a local deviation of the compass. The extent of these effects on the instrument can be obtained by comparing the observed variation with the variation given by chart. This deviation is compensated by placing magnets around the compass, in such a position as to produce the desired change in the direction of the compass needle.

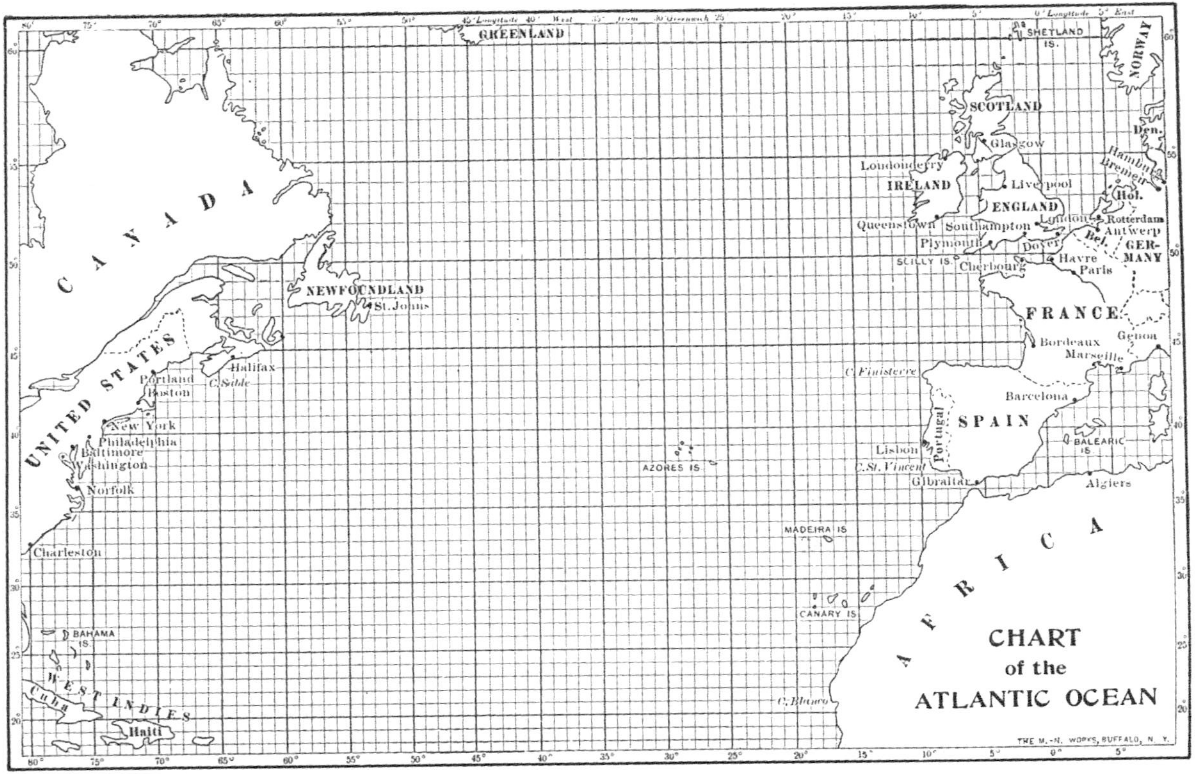
CHART
of the
ATLANTIC OCEAN
THE M.-N. WORKS, BUFFALO, N. Y.
CANADA
UNITED STATES
NEWFOUNDLAND
St. Johns
Halifax
C. Sable
Portland
Boston
New York
Philadelphia
Baltimore
Washington
Norfolk
Charleston
BAHAMA IS.
WEST INDIES
Cuba
Haiti
GREENLAND
AZORES IS.
MADEIRA IS.
CANARY IS.
C. Blanco
AFRICA
SHETLAND IS.
NORWAY
SCOTLAND
Glasgow
IRELAND
Londonderry
Queenstown
ENGLAND
Liverpool
London
Southampton
Plymouth
Dover
SCILLY IS.
Cherbourg
Havre
Paris
Den.
Hamburg
Bremen
Hol.
Rotterdam
Antwerp
Bel.
GERMANY
FRANCE
Bordeaux
Marseille
Genoa
C. Finisterre
SPAIN
Portugal
Barcelona
Lisbon
C. St. Vincent
Gibraltar
BALEARIC IS.
Algiers
45° Longitude 40° West 35° from 30° Greenwich 25°
0° Longitude 5° East

Sites & Excursions

Place Visited	Remarks

Sites & Excursions

Place Visited	Remarks
. . . .	. . . .
. . . .	. . . .
. . . .	. . . .
. . . .	. . . .
. . . .	. . . .
. . . .	. . . .
. . . .	. . . .
. . . .	. . . .
. . . .	. . . .
. . . .	. . . .
. . . .	. . . .
. . . .	. . . .
. . . .	. . . .
. . . .	. . . .
. . . .	. . . .
. . . .	. . . .
. . . .	. . . .
. . . .	. . . .
. . . .	. . . .
. . . .	. . . .

Sites & Excursions

PLACE VISITED	REMARKS
. . . .	. . . .
. . . .	. . . .
. . . .	. . . .
. . . .	. . . .
. . . .	. . . .
. . . .	. . . .
. . . .	. . . .
. . . .	. . . .
. . . .	. . . .
. . . .	. . . .
. . . .	. . . .
. . . .	. . . .
. . . .	. . . .
. . . .	. . . .
. . . .	. . . .
. . . .	. . . .
. . . .	. . . .
. . . .	. . . .
. . . .	. . . .
. . . .	. . . .

Sites & Excursions

Place Visited	Remarks

Sites & Excursions

Place Visited	Remarks

Sites & Excursions

Place Visited	Remarks
. . . .	. . . .
. . . .	. . . .
. . . .	. . . .
. . . .	. . . .
. . . .	. . . .
. . . .	. . . .
. . . .	. . . .
. . . .	. . . .
. . . .	. . . .
. . . .	. . . .
. . . .	. . . .
. . . .	. . . .
. . . .	. . . .
. . . .	. . . .
. . . .	. . . .
. . . .	. . . .
. . . .	. . . .
. . . .	. . . .
. . . .	. . . .
. . . .	. . . .

Sites & Excursions

Place Visited	Remarks

Sites & Excursions

Place Visited	Remarks

Sites & Excursions

Place Visited	Remarks

Major Mountains of the World

Name	Height (ft)	Location
Mount Everest	29,028	Tibet/Nepal
Qogir (K2)	28,250	Pakistan (Kashmir)
Kanchenjunga	28,208	Nepal
Makalu I	27,824	Tibet/Nepal
Dhaulagiri	26,810	Nepal
Manaslu I	26,760	Nepal
Cho Oyu	26,750	Tibet/Nepal
Nanga Parbat	26,660	Pakistan (Kashmir)
Annapurna I	26,504	Nepal
Gasherbrum	26,470	Kashmir
Broad Peak	26,400	Kashmir
Gosainthan	26,287	Tibet
Central Peak	26,284	Kashmir
Annapurna II	26,041	Nepal
Gyachung Kang	25,910	Tibet/Nepal
Disteghil Sar	25,868	Pakistan (Kashmir)
Himalchuli	25,801	Nepal
Masherbrum	25,660	Pakistan (Kashmir)
Nanda Devi	25,645	India
Rakaposhi	25,550	Pakistan (Kashmir)

Major Mountains of the World

Name	Height (ft)	Location
Kamet	25,447	Tibet/India
Namcha Barwa	25,445	Tibet
Gurla Mandhata	25,355	Tibet
Ulugh Muztagh	25,340	China
Kungur	25,325	China (Xinjiang)
Aconcagua	22,834	Argentina/Chile
Mount McKinley	20,320	USA (Alaska)
Kilimanjaro	19,340	Tanzania
Citlaltepetl (Orizaba)	18,700	Mexico
Elbrus	18,510	Russia
Mount Ararat	17,050	Turkey
Vinson Massif	16,864	Antarctica
Puncak Jaya	16,499	Indonesia
Mont Blanc	15,771	France/Italy
Mount Whitney	14,494	USA (California)
Mount Fuji	12,388	Japan
Mount Cook	12,349	New Zealand
Pico de Aneto	11,168	Spain
Olympus	9,570	Greece
Mount Sinai	7,497	Egypt

Longest Rivers of the World

Name	Length (mi)	Location
Nile	4,160	North/East Africa
Amazon	4,000	South America
Chang Jiang (Yangtze)	3,964	China
Huang He	3,395	China
Ob-Irtysh	3,362	Russia
Amur	2,744	Northeast Asia
Lena	2,734	Russia
Congo	2,718	Central Africa
Mackenzie	2,635	Canada
Mekong	2,600	Southeast Asia
Niger	2,590	Africa
Yenisey	2,543	Russia
Parana	2,485	South America
Mississippi	2,340	USA
Murray Darling	2,310	Australia
Volga	2,290	Russia
Sao Francisco	1,988	Brazil
Yukon	1,979	Alaska/Canada
Rio Grande	1,900	USA/Mexico
Brahmaputra	1,800	China/India

Islands of the World

Name	Area (mi²)	Name	Area (Mi²)
Greenland	822,700	Sri Lanka	25,332
New Guinea	309,000	Tasmania	24,868
Borneo	283,400	Tierra del Fuego	18,530
Madagascar	226,658	Kyushu (Japan)	14,114
Sumatra	167,600	Taiwan	13,851
Honshu (Japan)	87,805	Sicily	9,830
Victoria (Canada)	83,897	Sardinia	9,194
Great Britain	83,698	Jamaica	4,244
Celebes	69,100	Hawaii	4,028
South Island (NZ)	58,676	Cyprus	3,572
Java	49,000	Puerto Rico	3,435
North Island (NZ)	44,204	Corsica	3,351
Newfoundland	42,031	Crete	3,190
Cuba	40,519	Bali	2,147
Iceland	39,699	Long Island (NY)	1,401
Ireland	32,589	Zanzibar	640
Hokkaido (Japan)	30,144	Tahiti	402

Notes & Incidents

Notes & Incidents

Notes & Incidents

Notes & Incidents

Notes & Incidents

Notes & Incidents

Notes & Incidents

Notes & Incidents

Notes & Incidents

Notes & Incidents

Notes & Incidents

Notes & Incidents

Notes & Incidents

Notes & Incidents

Notes & Incidents

Notes & Incidents

Notes & Incidents

Notes & Incidents

Notes & Incidents

Notes & Incidents

Notes & Incidents

Notes & Incidents

Notes & Incidents

Notes & Incidents

Notes & Incidents

Notes & Incidents

Notes & Incidents

Notes & Incidents

Notes & Incidents

Notes & Incidents

Notes & Incidents

Notes & Incidents

Notes & Incidents

Notes & Incidents

Notes & Incidents

Notes & Incidents

Notes & Incidents

Notes & Incidents

Notes & Incidents

Notes & Incidents

Notes & Incidents

Notes & Incidents

Notes & Incidents

Notes & Incidents

Notes & Incidents

Notes & Incidents

Autographs & Sketches

Autographs & Sketches

Autographs & Sketches

Autographs & Sketches

Autographs & Sketches

Autographs & Sketches

Autographs & Sketches

Autographs & Sketches

Autographs & Sketches

Autographs & Sketches

Autographs & Sketches

Autographs & Sketches

Ephemera

[ticket stubs, restaurant receipts, etc.]

Ephemera

[ticket stubs, restaurant receipts, etc.]

Ephemera

[ticket stubs, restaurant receipts, etc.]

Ephemera

[ticket stubs, restaurant receipts, etc.]

Ephemera

[ticket stubs, restaurant receipts, etc.]

Ephemera

[ticket stubs, restaurant receipts, etc.]

Ephemera

[ticket stubs, restaurant receipts, etc.]

Ephemera

[ticket stubs, restaurant receipts, etc.]

Ephemera

[ticket stubs, restaurant receipts, etc.]

Ephemera

[ticket stubs, restaurant receipts, etc.]

Ephemera

[ticket stubs, restaurant receipts, etc.]

Ephemera

[ticket stubs, restaurant receipts, etc.]

Homeward Bound

Departing from: ....

Via: ....

Date: ....

Time of departure: ....

Time of arrival: ....

The wise man travels to discover himself.

—James Russell Lowell